Crabapples

HOW a plant grows

Bobbie Kalman

🌱 Crabtree Publishing Company

Crabapples

created by Bobbie Kalman

For Connie Warner, who loves plants

Editor-in-Chief
Bobbie Kalman

Research
Janine Schaub
Niki Walker

Writing team
Bobbie Kalman
Niki Walker

Managing editor
Lynda Hale

Editors
Greg Nickles
Petrina Gentile

Computer design
Lynda Hale

Color separations and film
Dot 'n Line Image Inc.

All illustrations by Barbara Bedell, except for:
Halina Below-Spada: page 31

Photographs
Peter Crabtree: page 4 (bottom left)
Bobbie Kalman: pages 4 (bottom right), 5 (all), 22, 23 (top right)
Dwight R. Kuhn: cover, pages 10, 15, 20 (top), 21, 23 (top left), 23 (bottom)
Diane Payton Majumdar: pages 16-17 (top), 16 (bottom), 20 (bottom), 27
Photo Researchers, Inc.: Dr. Jeremy Burgess/SPL: pages 11 (top), 16-17 (bottom); E.R. Degginger: page 25 (bottom); Michael P. Gadomski: page 12; Adam Hart-Davis/SPL: page 6; Stephen J. Krasemann: page 11 (bottom); J.H. Robinson: page 24 (top); Alvin E. Staffan: page 14; Jerome Wexler: page 24 (bottom); Dr. Paul Zahl: page 25 (top)
Richard Shiell: title page

Printer
Worzalla Publishing Company

Crabtree Publishing Company

350 Fifth Avenue
Suite 3308
New York
N.Y. 10118

360 York Road, RR 4,
Niagara-on-the-Lake,
Ontario, Canada
L0S 1J0

73 Lime Walk
Headington
Oxford OX3 7AD
United Kingdom

Cataloging in Publication Data
Kalman, Bobbie
  How a plant grows

(Crabapples)
Includes index.

ISBN 0-86505-628-5 (library bound)   ISBN 0-86505-728-1 (pbk.)
This book examines the stages of a seed plant's development—germination, photosynthesis, and pollination and includes activities on how to grow plants.

1. Growth (Plants) - Juvenile literature. 2. Plants - Development - Juvenile literature. 3. Growth (Plants) - Experiments - Juvenile literature. I. Title. II. Series: Kalman, Bobbie. Crabapples.

QK731.K335 1996   j581.3   LC 96-41202
                                                                                CIP

What is in this book?

What are plants? 4

Parts of a plant 6

The life of a seed plant 8

Coming to life 10

Making food 13

Flowers bloom 14

Flower visitors 17

Making seeds 18

Seeds on the move 20

Other ways plants start 22

Meat eaters 24

Why plants are important 26

Try these activities 28

Words to know & Index 32

What are plants?

Plants are living things. They are the only living things that can make their own food. Plants cannot move from place to place as animals can. They stay in the same spot their whole life. Plants live in soil, sand, snow, and rock. Some even grow on top of other plants!

Trees, shrubs, and ferns are plants.

Some plants grow in water.

Most plants have roots, leaves, flowers, and a stem. Many grow from seeds. This book looks at how these plants grow.

Many plants have colorful flowers.

Fruit contains the seeds of a plant.

Plants can grow almost anywhere!

Parts of a plant

Green plants have three parts:
a stem, roots, and leaves. Each
part of the plant has important
jobs to do.

The stem holds up
the leaves and flowers.
It carries water and
minerals from the roots
to the leaves. Food made
in the leaves travels down
the stem to the roots.

Roots hold the plant in
place. They absorb water
and **minerals** from the soil
for the plant to use. Plants
need minerals to grow.
Roots also store extra food.

Leaves catch sunlight and use it to make food for the plant. The plant's wastes are also stored in its leaves. When leaves fall off, they take the waste with them.

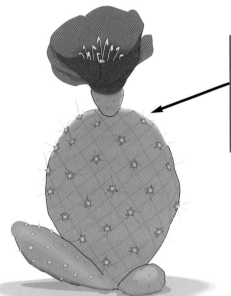

Not all leaves are wide and flat. The needles on cactus plants and evergreen trees are thin, waxy leaves.

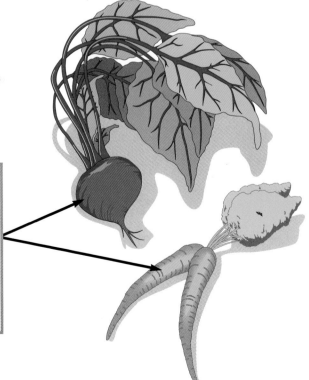

Some vegetables, such as carrots, radishes, and beets, are roots. They store food for the plant to use over the winter. They also give the plant energy to grow a new stem and leaves in the spring.

The life of a seed plant

These pictures show how a bean plant grows from a seed. Some plants, such as beans, take less than one year to go through these stages, or **life cycle**, before they die. They are called **annuals**. **Biennials**, such as carrots, take two years to finish their life cycle.

Perennials, such as trees, bushes, and many flowers, live for at least three years.

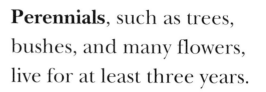

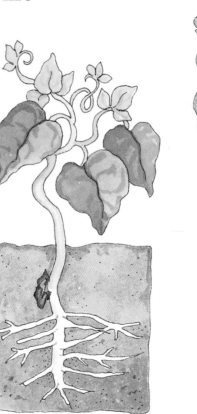

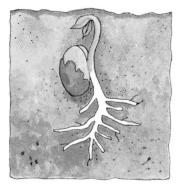

1. The seed breaks open. A root grows down into the soil, and a stem grows upward.

2. The small young plant, or **seedling**, grows leaves and can make its own food.

3. When the plant is fully grown, it makes flowers. Insects or birds visit the flowers.

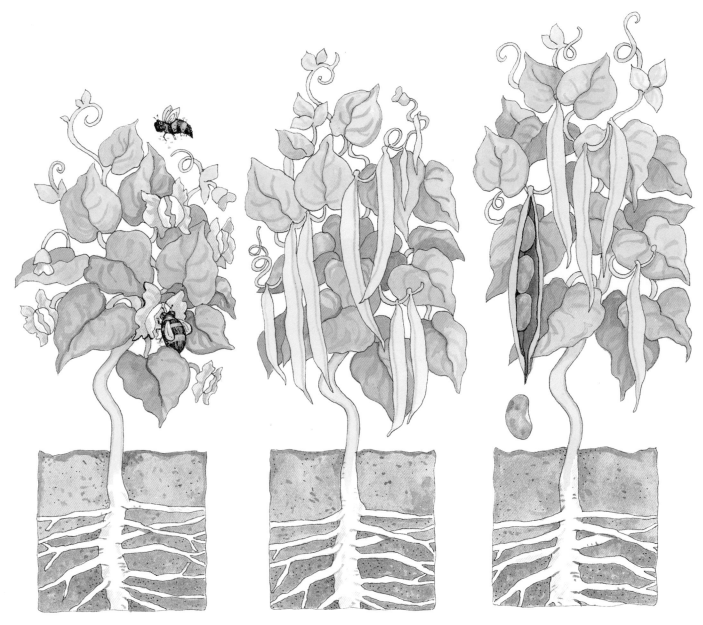

4. They bring parts of other flowers with them. The plant can now make seeds.

5. The flower dies and seeds grow inside it. A fruit forms around the seeds.

6. The seeds fall from the plant so they have room to grow. They become new plants.

Coming to life

Inside each seed is a tiny plant waiting to grow, or **germinate**. Seeds will not sprout if they do not have enough heat and water. Some seeds can wait for one hundred years before they sprout!

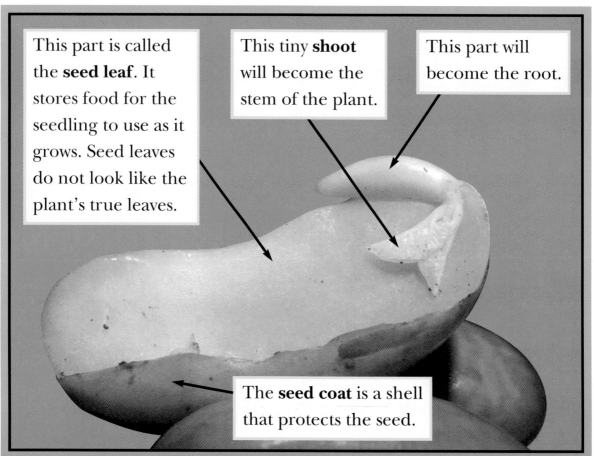

This part is called the **seed leaf**. It stores food for the seedling to use as it grows. Seed leaves do not look like the plant's true leaves.

This tiny **shoot** will become the stem of the plant.

This part will become the root.

The **seed coat** is a shell that protects the seed.

When a seed germinates, a tiny root breaks through the seed coat and pushes down into the soil. Then a tiny shoot grows upward. After the shoot pushes up through the soil, the seed leaves shrivel. The seedling has used up all the food stored inside. As the seed leaves disappear, the plant's true leaves appear.

Making food

When a seedling grows true leaves, it begins making its own food. Making food is called **photosynthesis**.

Not all plants are able to make their own food. Only plants with **chlorophyll** in their leaves can make food. Chlorophyll gives leaves their green color. It uses the sun's energy to turn air and water into a sugar called **glucose**. The plant uses glucose as food.

The leaves of some trees change color in the autumn. They change because there is not enough light, and the chlorophyll that makes them green is destroyed. The leaves can no longer make food. The tree uses stored food through autumn and winter.

Flowers bloom

More than half of all plants have flowers. Most flowers are brightly colored and have a scent. Some are small, green, and have no smell. Trees and grasses have small flowers that have no scent.

Flowers have different looks and smells, but they all do the same job. They help with **pollination** and making seeds. Pollination happens when the pollen from one plant reaches another plant of the same kind. After pollination takes place, seeds can be made.

Flowers with brightly colored **petals** attract birds and insects.

Stamens are around the **pistil** in the middle of the flower. Stamens are covered with dusty powder called **pollen**.

stigma

pistil

The sticky top of the pistil is called the **stigma**. When pollen from another flower gets stuck on its stigma, a flower is pollinated.

Flower visitors

Most flowers need **pollinators** to move their pollen to other plants. Pollinators are visitors such as bees, birds, and bugs. They visit colorful flowers that have strong scents. Many of these flowers have **nectar** inside. Nectar is a sweet liquid that some pollinators like to drink.

While drinking nectar, the pollinators get covered with pollen grains. When they visit another plant, the pollen brushes off onto its flower. The flower is pollinated, and seeds can be made.

Some plants, such as trees and grasses, use the wind to move their pollen. Their flowers are not large or colorful because they do not need to attract pollinators.

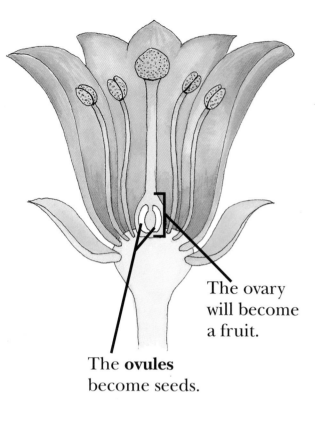

The ovary will become a fruit.

The **ovules** become seeds.

Making seeds

After a flower is pollinated, seeds begin to grow inside it. Its petals fall off. The **ovary** inside the flower grows larger and becomes a **fruit**. A fruit is the part of the plant that has seeds inside.

The petals fall off.

The ovary grows larger.

These apple blossoms have been pollinated.

There are many different types of fruits. Some, such as pea pods and watermelon, have many seeds inside. Others, such as cherries and plums, have only one seed.

Some fruits are soft and juicy. Peaches, raspberries, and tomatoes are examples of these fruits. Other fruits, such as those around peanuts and sunflower seeds, are thin, dry, and hard.

The ovary finally becomes an apple, and the ovules have become the seeds.

The ovary gets bigger as the seeds grow inside.

Seeds on the move

Once seeds are made, they need places to grow. Animals, wind, and water help move the seeds of plants.

Many seeds are inside colorful, tasty fruit. When an animal eats the fruit, it also eats the seeds. Later, the seeds are scattered in the animal's droppings.

Seeds can also be carried by wind or water. Maple seeds, for example, have wings and fly like small helicopters. Dandelion seeds have parachutes to float away on a breeze. Some seeds, such as coconuts, float on water and sail to their new homes.

A few plants can scatter seeds without help. Some make their seeds inside fruits that burst open and spray the seeds all around. Others have fruits that are like rattles. Their seeds spill out when the fruits are shaken.

Some seeds are covered in tiny hooks that catch on animal fur. An animal carries the seed with it until the hooks break. The seeds then drop onto their home and become new plants.

21

Other ways plants start

Not all plants begin as seeds. Some grow from **bulbs**. Others, such as ferns and mosses, grow from tiny specks called **spores**.

Plants that do grow seeds can make new plants in other ways. Some, such as trees and rose bushes, send up small shoots, or **suckers**, from their roots.

The suckers become new plants. Other trees begin as roots. The tropical tree below is sending down new roots from its branches. When the roots reach the ground, they become new trunks that grow into trees. These trees look more like a forest than a single tree.

Some trees grow roots from their branches.

Some plants grow from bulbs.

Some plants start as suckers.

Some plants grow from spores.

Meat eaters

Some plants are **carnivorous**. They eat meat. They do make some of their own food, but they cannot get enough nutrients from the swampy soil where they live. They get more nutrients by eating insects.

The Venus flytrap has leaves with long bristles. When an insect touches these bristles, the leaf snaps shut around it!

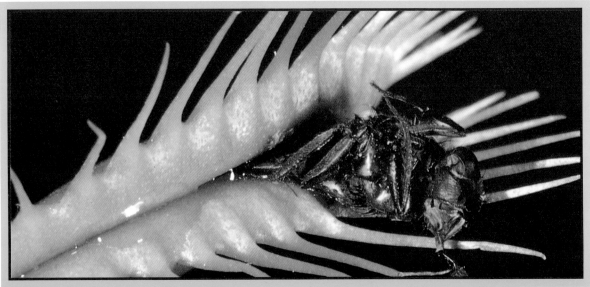

A pitcher plant has leaves that are like slippery jugs filled with juice. Insects slip down the side of a leaf and drown in the liquid at the bottom. Hairs that point downwards stop the insect from crawling out. The plant's juices then turn the insect to liquid, which the plant uses as food.

Why plants are important

People and other creatures cannot live without plants. Plants take energy from the sun and use it to turn water and air into food. The energy is passed on to other creatures when they eat the plant's root, leaves, stem, or fruit.

Some creatures do not eat plants, but they eat the animals that feed on plants. The food energy that started with a plant gets passed along the food chain and keeps other creatures alive.

People use plants for food, but they also need them for other things. Medicine, clothes, and furniture are made from plants.

Other creatures need plants, too. Fields and forests are home to many types of animals. The plants give animals shelter from the weather and help them hide from enemies. Plants also make the air fresher. They produce **oxygen**, a gas that humans and animals need to breathe.

Try these activities

Grow a bean plant!

You will need:

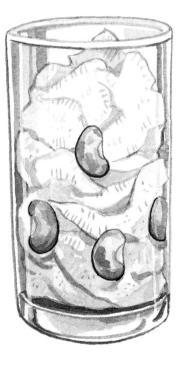

- a glass
- paper towels
- water
- a few dried beans
- a plastic container such as an ice cream tub
- potting soil

1. Soak dried beans in water overnight.
2. Scrunch up paper towels and stuff them into a glass.
3. Add enough water to soak the paper towels.
4. Place the beans between the glass and the paper towels. Space the beans at least 1 inch (2.5 cm) apart.

5. Put the jar in a warm, dark place such as a cupboard. Make sure the paper towels stay damp. Watch for a tiny root to sprout after a few days.

6. Soon after the root sprouts, a small stem will grow up towards the top of the glass.

7. When your seedling is about 2 inches (5 cm) tall, you can plant it in soil placed in the container.

8. In about ten days, the stem of the plant will have grown its true leaves. Now your plant is making its own food!

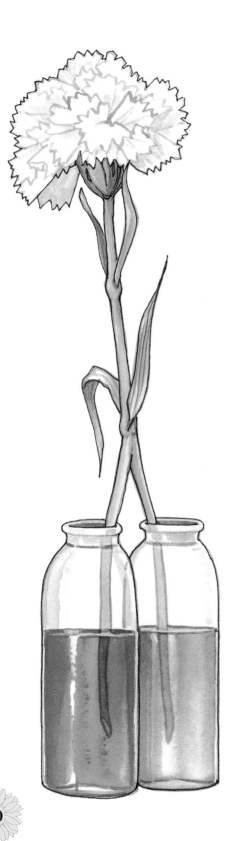

Watch a plant drink!

You will need:

- a white carnation with a long, thick stem (get one from a flower shop)
- 2 small, clear bottles or narrow glasses
- water
- red food coloring
- blue food coloring
- a paring knife
- an adult to help you use the knife

1. Fill the bottles or glasses with water.
2. Add a few drops of red food coloring to one bottle and drops of blue to the other.
3. With an adult's help, cut the stem starting from the bottom, until the flower will stand up in the bottles.
4. Put half the stem in the bottle with red coloring and the other half in the bottle with blue.
5. Leave your flower and bottles in a sunny spot for a few hours and then check them. What did you find?

Make an indoor garden!

You will need:

🍁 3 or 4 small house plants that need the same amount of light and water—plants that grow in warm, wet environments are the easiest to use

🍁 a glass container such as a small aquarium or a large jar with a big opening

🍁 potting soil

🍁 gravel

🍁 a spoon

🍁 spray bottle

1. Cover the bottom of a container with a layer of gravel.

2. Put a layer of soil on top of the gravel. Make sure that the soil is deep enough to allow the plant roots to grow.

3. Wet the soil.

4. With the spoon, dig out holes and place the plants in them.

5. Cover the roots with soil and place your container in a well-lit place.

6. With a spray bottle, keep the plants and soil moist, but not wet. Watch them grow.

Words to know

bulb A round, underground part of a plant from which a new plant grows

chlorophyll The substance in leaves that makes them green and allows them to make food

germinate To begin to grow

minerals Crystals found in the soil that nourish plants

nectar A sweet liquid made in many flowers, used by bees to make honey

ovary The part of a flower that becomes a fruit

ovules The parts of a flower, found inside the ovary, which become seeds

photosynthesis The process by which green plants make food

pollination The movement of pollen from one flower to another of the same kind

seed leaves The parts of a seed that store food for the seedling to use as it grows

seedling A young plant that grows from a seed

shoot A new or young growth on a plant

spore A dustlike part of some plants, from which a new plant may grow

sucker A shoot that grows from roots or the underground part of a stem

true leaves Leaves that replace the seed leaves and make food

Index

animals 4, 20, 21, 26, 27
birds 8, 15, 17
bulbs 22, 23
experiments 28-31
flowers 5, 6, 8, 9, 14-15, 17, 18, 30
food 4, 6, 7, 8, 10, 11, 13, 24, 25, 26, 29
food chain 26
fruit 5, 9, 18-19, 20, 26
germination 10-11
insects 8, 15, 17, 24, 25
leaves 5, 6, 7, 8, 10, 11, 13, 24, 25, 26, 29
photosynthesis 13
pollen 14, 15, 17
pollination 14, 15, 17, 18
pollinators 17
roots 5, 6, 7, 8, 10, 11, 22, 26, 29, 31
seedling 8, 10, 11, 13, 29
seeds 5, 8, 9, 10, 11, 14, 17, 18-19, 20-21, 22
soil 4, 6, 8, 11, 24, 28, 29, 31
spores 22, 23
stem 5, 6, 7, 8, 10, 26, 29, 30
sunlight 7, 13, 26, 31
trees 4, 7, 8, 13, 14, 17, 22
water 4, 6, 10, 13, 20, 26, 28, 30, 31

1 2 3 4 5 6 7 8 9 0 Printed in USA 6 5 4 3 2 1 0 9 8 7